MORE THAN 500 OF THE MOST RUTHLESS, RAW, AND HARD-
CORE SNAPS, CAPS, AND DISSES FROM THE OFFICIAL SNAPPING
SOURCE, CELEBRITIES, AND MASTER SNAPPERS ON THE STREET

SNAPS4

JAMES PERCELAY

SNAPS4

DON'T BE OUT-SNAPPED!

MAKE SURE YOU OWN . . .

SNAPS, DOUBLE SNAPS, & TRIPLE SNAPS BY

SNAPS 4

JAMES PERCELAY

QUILL
WILLIAM MORROW
NEW YORK

It is the policy of William Morrow and Company, Inc., and its
imprints and affiliates, recognizing the importance of preserving
what has been written, to print the books we publish on acid-
free paper, and we exert our best efforts to that end.

Library of Congress Cataloging-in-Publication Data

Percelay, James
  Snaps 4 / James Percelay.
    p. cm.
  ISBN 0-688-15014-4
  1. Afro-American wit and humor. 2. Invective—Humor.
I. Percelay, James. II. Title.
PN6231.N5P47 1998
818'.5402—dc21   97-24140
                                            CIP

Printed in the United States of America

First Edition

1 2 3 4 5 6 7 8 9 10

BOOK DESIGN BY ELIZABETH VAN ITALLIE

www.williammorrow.com

4

DEDICATED TO
MY FAMILY AND FRIENDS

To Doris Cooper and Will Schwalbe, thanks for being there.

Special thanks to . . .
Monteria Ivey and Stephan Dweck

Contributing Editor
Michelle Cuccuini

Also thanks to
Frank Weimann / The Literary Group,
Rob Wolken, The William Morris Agency,
Brandon Tartikoff, Kim Fleary, Richard Kline

CONTENTS

6

7

WIL SYLVINCE

GERALD KELLY

SNAPPING RULES

1. DON'T TOUCH YOUR OPPONENT.

2. USE A REFEREE.

3. SNAP IN FRONT OF A CROWD.

4. DON'T SPIT.

ARDIE FUQUA

JAMES WYATT LAWRENCE

9

STUPID

SNAPS

10

Your girlfriend is so stupid, she bought training wheels for her menstrual cycle.

Your mother is so stupid, she thought **INNUENDO** was an Italian suppository.

Your brother is so dumb, he thinks Cheerios are doughnut seeds.

Your mother so dumb, she thinks giving birth is "making a living."

You're so dumb, you thought the **MILLION MAN MARCH** was a Lotto game.

Your girlfriend is so dumb, she thought foreplay was a skit.

You're so stupid, you think a dumbwaiter is somebody who
MESSES UP YOUR ORDER.

Your mother is so stupid, she called the cocaine hot line to order some.

Your brother is so stupid, he went to the drive-in to see *Closed for Winter.*

YOUR FATHER IS SO DUMB, he turned himself in to collect the reward money.

Your mother is so dumb, SHE CUT OFF HER HAND to give someone the finger.

You're so dumb, you think Puffy Combs is a cereal.

You're so stupid, you thought Wu-Tang was AN ASIAN ORANGE DRINK.

You're so stupid, when you graduated kindergarten you got so excited you cut yourself shaving.

Your sister is so dumb, she thinks a traffic jam is a block party.

YOU'RE SO DUMB, YOU THINK **LL COOL J HAS A** STUTTERING PROBLEM.

Your mother is so stupid, she told everyone she was "illegitimate" because she couldn't read.

Your sister is so dumb, she thinks Kotex is a radio station in Texas.

Your mother is so dumb, she wouldn't let you watch BET because **SHE THOUGHT IT WAS GAMBLING.**

Your sister is so stupid, she got hit by a coffee cup and told the cops she got mugged.

Your mother is so stupid, she got stuck on an escalator.

Your mother is so stupid, IT TOOK HER A MONTH to get rid of a seven-day itch.

Your mother is so stupid, she thought Johnny Cash was a pay toilet.

Your girl is so stupid, she tried to rub the dot off an Indian woman to see what prize she had won.

Your father is so stupid, you have to dig for his IQ.

Your brother is so dumb, he wonders why he has an ORANGE DICK when his job is watching pornos and eating Chee•tos

Your sister is so dumb, when I asked her to talk dirty she said,
"Mud, grease, garbage . . ."

Your mother is so dumb, she went to the beauty salon with a bag of
snakes talkin' about **"GETTING A MEDUSA."**

Your mother is so dumb, she knocked on her door to get out.

You're so stupid, you called a travel agency to find "Gangsta's Paradise."

Your sister is so dumb, when your mother lost weight she went
looking for it.

You're so stupid, your underwear is Fruit of the **LOONY.**

Your brother is so dumb, I told him to take a picture so he stole a painting.

Your father is so dumb, he thought Fixodent was an auto body shop.

YOUR SISTER IS SO STUPID, when she got rich she went and bought a mint.

Your mother is so dumb, when you said, "Christmas is right around the corner," she looked.

YOU'RE SO DUMB, YOU THINK YOUR *EX*-GIRLFRIEND IS A MUSLIM.

Your mother is so stupid, when she goes into an elevator it turns into a dumbwaiter.

Your mother is so stupid, SHE THOUGHT GAN-GRENE was a golf course for bums.

Your mother is so stupid, she tried to read an audio book.

Your mother is so stupid, she returned a puzzle saying it was broken.

Your mother is so stupid, SHE SAT ON A WINDOW LEDGE thinking she'd get framed

Your mother is so stupid, she watches *The Three Stooges* and takes notes.

Your mother is so stupid, she went to a Whalers game to see Shamu.

Your mother is so stupid, she went to **ALPHA BETA** and asked to buy a vowel.

Your mother is so stupid, she went to a baseball game and drowned in a wave.

Your mother is so stupid, she cut her head to keep an open mind.

YOUR MOTHER IS SO STUPID, SHE THOUGHT LIONEL RICHIE WAS A WEALTHY KID WITH TRAINS.

Your mother is so stupid, on a job application under "Sex?" she wrote "Yes."

Your father is so stupid, HE BOUGHT A VIDEO CAMERA to tape TV shows at home.

Your mother is so dumb, she got arrested for battering shrimp.

Your mother is so stupid, she was born on Independence Day but can't REMEMBER HER BIRTHDAY.

Your brother is so stupid, he thought a 69er was a football team.

Your daddy is illiterate, so what's he talkin' 'bout "LET ME SPELL IT OUT FOR YA"?

Your mother is so dumb, she's missing a finger and can't count past nine.

Your father is so stupid, he had your brother beat up his car because it needed a jump.

You're so stupid, when you were young you needed lessons on HOW TO MASTURBATE.

Your sister is so dumb, she thinks getting knocked up is a promotion.

Your mother is so stupid, she wore a helmet in Kmart in case she got hit by falling prices.

Your brother is so stupid, he thinks a scholarship is a sailboat with teachers on it.

Your mother is so dumb, I told her there was a **CHANGE IN THE WEATHER** so she ran to get her purse.

Your mother is so dumb, she thinks Eazy E is a laxative.

Your mother is so dumb, she mends your clothes with a stapler.

Your brother is so dumb, he threw a fit at a gumball machine because it wouldn't take food stamps.

You're so stupid, I locked you in a bathroom and you shit in your pants.

Your sister is so stupid, when she was told a statue was erected in town she asked HOW LONG IT WAS.

You're so stupid, you think "Tutti-Frutti" is a gay trumpet player.

Your girlfriend is so stupid, during oral sex I asked if she wanted some "man milk" and she said, "No, I'm lactose-intolerant."

Your mother is so stupid, she thinks **A BIG GULP** is swallowing from a fat guy.

Your father is so stupid, when his Army sergeant yelled, "Incoming, everybody get down!" he jumped up and started dancing.

Your mother is so dumb, she thought Coolio was a soft drink.

You're so dumb, you think Samsonite is a character in the Bible.

Your mother is so stupid, **SHE PUT ON SCUBA GEAR** to see *Waiting to Exhale*.

Your brother is so dumb, he brought **A BIRD FEEDER** to an Atlanta Hawks game.

Your sister is so dumb, she wore a raincoat to a Tampa Bay Lightning game.

YOUR IS SO DUMB, A HICKEY IS SEVEN

Your brother is so stupid, she brought a flyswatter to a Charlotte Hornets game.

MOTHER

Your father is so dumb, he thinks "higher education" is buying his alphabet soup from off the top shelf.

SHE THINKS ONE OF THE DWARFS.

Your brother is so dumb, he thinks Immaculate Conception is when your girl takes a shower.

Your mother is so dumb, when her boss told her to retire she went out and BOUGHT FOUR MICHELINS.

Your girlfriend is so stupid, she has to open her blouse to count to two.

You're so stupid, you think Cheez Whiz is ONLY FOR SMART PEOPLE.

Your sister is so dumb, she thinks Chernobyl is Cher's full name.

Your mother is so dumb, she flunked a sign language class because she couldn't hear the teacher.

Your sister is so dumb, she thought B.V.D. was a cable channel.

Your sister is so stupid, she thought a microwave is **A HAIR-STYLE FOR MIDGETS.**

Your sister is so dumb, she took a towel to a baby shower.

Your mother is so stupid, she thought **A SEPTIC TANK** was what Iraq invaded Kuwait with.

Your mother is so dumb, she slid a phone down her pants to make a booty call.

Your sister is so dumb, she went to the Department of Labor when she was pregnant.

Your mother is so stupid, she gets P M S *after* her period.

Your sister is so dumb, she thought "apartheid" means to spread your legs.

Your mother is so stupid, she tried to build a solar-powered windmill.

Your mother is so stupid, she tried to buy a vowel on *Jeopardy!*

Your mother is so dumb, SHE BURNED DOWN THE HOUSE making Kool-Aid.

Your mother is so stupid she thought "socialism" was ebonics for "partying."

Your mother is so stupid, she tried to whistle to make her Clapper work.

Your mother is so stupid, she tried to jam a James Brown 45 into your CD player.

Your brother is so dumb, he won't touch a TV screen because he's afraid the colors will rub off.

Your sister is so dumb, she ate a three-course meal, then asked the waiter for a grade.

You're so dumb, you thought HEAVY D was a bra size.

Your mother is so stupid, she tried to whistle to make her Clapper work.

You're so dumb, you'd have to go to school to BECOME AN IDIOT.—EDDIE GRIFFIN, *MALCOLM AND EDDIE*

YOU'RE SO DUMB, YOU THINK KOOL-AID IS WHAT ESKIMOS GET FROM UNSAFE SEX.

Your father is so dumb, when I asked him what the three hardest years in school were he said, "FIRST GRADE."

Your father is so dumb, he thought a section eight was where he parked his car.

UGLY
SNAPS

Your mother is so ugly, she's an extra on *The Simpsons.*

You're so ugly, after breast-feeding your mother used to **BOIL HER NIPPLES.**

Your girlfriend is so ugly, when Arnold Schwarzenegger stepped up to her he said, "I won't be back!"

Your mother is so ugly, she could curdle piss.

You're so ugly, when you were a baby your mom wiped your face **AND BREAST-FED YOUR ASS.**

Your mother is so ugly, she practices birth control by leaving the **LIGHTS ON.**

Your mother is so ugly, when they said, "she was ugly as sin," sin sued.

If ugliness was gas, you'd have a full tank.

Your mother is so ugly, she looks like she's been **BOBBING FOR FRENCH FRIES.**

Your mother is so ugly, it looks like she sleeps on a bed of nails facedown.

Your father is so ugly, he's on *America's Most Unwanted.*

Your mother is so ugly, she looks like a bulldog LICKING PISS OFF A THISTLE.

40 Your mother is so ugly, when she walks into the kitchen rats jump up on the chairs.

Your sister is so ugly, she couldn't sell her body at a rummage sale.

Your mother is so ugly, when she moons people THEY TURN INTO WEREWOLVES.

You're so ugly, your mom named you **JEAN-CLAUDE VAN** *DAMN.*

Your mother is so ugly, a fly wouldn't sit on her.

Your mother is so ugly, her dentist treats her by mail.

YOUR MOTHER IS SO UGLY, her face looks like a melted willy.

Your girlfriend is so ugly, the only time she got whistled at was just before a train hit her.

If my dog had a face as ugly as your mother's, I'd shave her ass and make her walk backward.

Your mother is so ugly, she ran after the mailman and got sprayed WITH MACE.

YOUR
IS SO UGLY,
HER IN'
CURE SEX

IF UGLINESS WERE A PAINTING, your mother would be a masterpiece.

MOTHER

Your family is so ugly, when they sit down for dinner it looks like the barroom scene from *Star Wars*.

THEY USE PRISONS TO OFFENDERS.

Your mother is so ugly, she's Freddy's nightmare.

Your mother is so ugly, she just got a job **AT THE AIR-PORT** sniffing drugs.

Your mother is so ugly, she could make a freight train take a gravel road.

Your mother is so ugly, people go as her for Halloween.

Your mother is so ugly, **I'VE SEEN COW PIES** I'd rather do it with.

Your mother is so ugly, she could scare the moss off a rock.

Your mother is so ugly, **SHE GETS 364 DAYS** to dress up for Halloween.

Your mother is so ugly, she has a face that could sink a thousand ships.

Your sister is so ugly, her favorite snack is Milk-Bones.

Your father is so ugly, he looks like the Elephant Man **CHEW-ING ON A WASP.**

You're so ugly, when your mother first saw you SHE GOT MORNING SICKNESS.

Your mother is so ugly, she scares roaches away.

Your mother is so ugly, she tried to take a bath and the water jumped out.

Your mother is so ugly, she turned Medusa to stone.

Your mother is so ugly, when she looked at a glass of milk IT TURNED TO CHEESE.

YOUR MOTHER IS SO UGLY, SHE WON'T EVEN PLAY WITH HERSELF.

Your mother is so ugly, she makes my ass pucker.

Your mother is so ugly, your daddy **WOULD RATHER KISS HER ASS** than her face.

Your mother is so ugly, you can tell it's her face only because it has ears.

Your mother is so ugly, they didn't give her a costume when she tried out for *Star Wars*.

You're so ugly, you went bungee-jumping and they put the cord around your neck.

Your girlfriend is so ugly, they pay her to **PUT HER CLOTHES ON** in strip joints.

Your mother is so ugly, when they took her to the beautician it took twelve hours just for a quote.

Your mother is so ugly, the psychiatrist makes her lie facedown.

You're so ugly, when you were born the doctor cried wolf.

Your baby's mother is so ugly, she could put the bogey man **OUT OF BUSINESS.**

YOUR MOTHER IS SO UGLY, SHE LOOKED INTO A WATER PUDDLE AND IT STARTED TO BOIL.

You're so ugly, I thought I'd seen the last of you when I flushed the toilet this morning.

Your father is so ugly, when he was arrested they sent him to an animal shelter.

Your mother is so ugly, she got thrown out of a store because the sign said **NO DOGS ALLOWED.**

Your sister is so ugly, she makes road kill get up and run away.

You're so ugly, your face is closed on weekends.

You're so ugly, in your yearbook photo they put black tape over your eyes.

Your sister is so ugly, her bath toy was an electric toaster.

Your mother is so ugly, your father calls her Libby because he met her at the pound.

Your mother is so ugly, I wouldn't do her with A STOLEN DICK.

Your parents are so ugly, their towels say "Hers" and "What."

YOUR BROTHER IS SO UGLY, McDONALD'S WON'T LET HIM SERVE HAPPY MEALS.

Your mother is so ugly, she has to GET HER VIBRATOR DRUNK FIRST.

Your mother is so ugly, she's a hostess at a Roach Motel.

FAT
SNAPS

55

Your mother is so fat, she uses bacon for Band-Aids.

Your mother is so fat, she keeps her diaphragm IN A PIZZA BOX.

Your father is so fat, he packs his lunch in his belly button.

YOUR MOTHER IS SO FAT, she masturbates with a telephone pole.

Your parents are so fat, when they have sex the Clapper goes on and off.

Your mother is so fat, SHE USES A BOOM BOX for a vibrator.

You're so fat, you jumped for joy and people yelled, "Eclipse!"

Your mother is so fat, they have to grease the door and dangle a Twinkies just to get her outside.

Your father is so fat, he has shocks on his toilet seat.

Your mother is so fat, she thinks A BALANCED MEAL is a ham in each hand.

YOUR MOTHER IS SO FAT, WHEN SHE' SINGS IT'S OVER.

Your mother is so fat, she thinks Church's Chicken is a holy place.

Your mother is so fat, she can't make it through the arches at McDonald's.

Your mother is so fat, **SHE USES A BLIMP** for a vibrator.

Your sister is so fat, to clean tunnels they tie a rope around her neck and drag her through.

Your mother is so fat, she uses a midget for a beeper.

Your mother is so fat, WHEN SHE FARTS it makes hurri-canes.

Your're so fat, you're the godfather of soul food. —MALCOLM JAMAL WARNER, *MALCOLM AND EDDIE*

Your girlfriend is so fat, she uses buses for Rollerblades.

Your mother is so fat, when she walks she looks like Jell-O jigglers.

Your mother is so fat, you can't tell WHERE HER TITS END and her arms begin.

Your mother is so fat, she wears a microwave for a beeper.

Your mother is so fat, she tells time by the meal: breakfast, lunch, dinner, and midnight snack.

Your girlfriend is so fat, SHE WAS PICKED AS BEST FLOAT in the Macy's Parade.

Your mother is so fat, she ate the Michelin Man thinking he was the Pillsbury Doughboy.

Your sister is so fat, Twinkies asked her to be its mascot.

Your mother is so fat, she's in the *Guinness Book* for eating the most *Guinness Books.*

Your mother is so fat, she uses redwoods to pick her teeth.

Your mother is so fat, she sat in my car and THE AIR BAG BLEW OUT.

Your mother is so fat, she sat on a rainbow and made skittles.
—WHOOPI GOLDBERG, *SISTER ACT II*

Your mother is so fat, she was Miss Arizona—Battleship Class.

YOUR MOTHER IS SO FAT, SHE BUTTERS HER TOAST WITH A PAINT ROLLER.

Your mother is so fat, animals at the zoo feed *her*.

Your mother is so fat, when she hugs herself she sings "We Are the World."

Your mother is so fat, HER PICTURE KEEPS FALLING OFF THE WALL.

Your mother is so fat, she wears a ghetto bra: It's as big as a project and has a hood on it.

Your mother is so fat, she works in the movies—as the screen.

Your mother's butt is so big, she uses the Astrodome for under-wear.

You're so fat, **WHEN YOU BUNGEE-JUMPED** you took the bridge with you.

Your mother is so fat, when she sweats your family opens umbrellas.

Your sister is so fat, she's got TB—two bellies.

Your mother is so fat, you can't tell if **SHE'S COMING OR GOING.**

YOUR MOTHER IS SO FAT, WHEN YOU PUT HER IN A JACUZZI SHE MAKES HER OWN GRAVY

Your mother is so fat, she has more rolls than a LITTLE DEBBIE'S TRUCK.

Your mother is so fat, running around her is an Olympic event.

Your mother is so fat, God couldn't light the earth until she stepped aside.

Your mother is so fat, NASA orbits a satellite around her.

Your mother is so fat, kids TRY TO RIDE HER at Great Adventure.

Your mother is so fat, when she rides in a hot-air balloon it looks like she's wearing tights.

Your sister is so fat, when I tried to drive around her I ran out of gas.

Your mother is so fat, she goes to the drive-in free because they THINK SHE'S A CHEVROLET.

Your mother is so fat, she can tag team wrestle by herself.

Your mother is so fat, when she wears a yellow jacket kids get on her for school.

Your mother is so fat and wet, they call her the LOVE BOAT.

Your mother is so fat, when she goes to a buffet they have to install speed bumps.

Your mother is so fat, she's like the Energizer Bunny: She keeps on eating and eating and eating. . . .

Your mother is so fat, when she stands in a left-turn lane it gives her THE GREEN ARROW.

Your father is so fat and white, he gets confused for the Michelin Man.

Youir mother is so fat, she went to Sizzler and got a group discount.

—DAVE CHAPELLE, *THE NUTTY PROFESSOR*

Your sister is so fat, at night your father puts the Club on the refrigerator.

You're so fat, they made a movie about your farts: *Twister!*

You're so fat, **IF IT WEREN'T FOR YOU** McDonald's would have only "400 Served."

Your mother is so fat, I sat on her lap and almost drowned.

Your mother is so fat, when I got on top of her I said, "Wow, I can see my house from here!"

Your mother is so fat, when she fell **ON 125TH STREET** people felt it **ON WEST 4TH.**

Your girlfriend is so fat, her shadow weighs more than you do.

You're so fat, they're going have to bury you in a **DOUBLE-DECKER COFFIN.**

Your father is so fat, he puts on his belt with a boomerang.

Your sister is so fat, WHEN SHE WENT INSIDE A GAP it filled in.

Your sister is so fat, she shops at Pigs "R" Us.

Your sister is so fat, she stepped on a rainbow and made skid marks.

Your mother is so fat, when she swims in the ocean, ship captains yell, "LAND HO!"

Your sister is so fat, she was baptized in gravy.

YOUR MOTHER IS SO FAT, SHE HAS TO GET OUT OF THE CAR TO SHIFT GEARS.

Your mother is so fat, buildings fall when she shakes her booty.

You're so fat, you must be on that new diet "Slim Show."

YOUR MOTHER IS SO FAT, she uses boom boxes and a rope for headphones.

Your mother is so fat, she gets her toenails painted at Earl Scheib.
—EDDIE MURPHY, *THE NUTTY PROFESSOR*

Your sister is so fat, they had to cut the Goodyear blimp in half to make her a bra.

I'm so fat, my sign is CAUTION WIDE LOAD.

—JAIME CARDRICHE, *MALCOLM AND EDDIE*

Your father is so fat, when he walks in a bowling alley the pins fall down.

OLD
SNAPS

Your mother is so old, she was the DJ at the **BOSTON TEA PARTY.**

Your mother is so old, she was at the First Supper.

Your mother is so old, she was born when **THE DEAD SEA** was only sick.

Your mother is so old, she's got more toes than teeth.

YOUR MOTHER IS SO OLD, on Wednesdays she gets a 100 percent discount.

YOUR FATHER IS SO OLD, HE HAS THE PATENT FOR FIRE.

Your mother is so old, her dreams are in black-and-white.

Your father is so old, they call him O.J. because it takes him eight months to get off.

Your mother is so old, the **THREE WISE MEN** helped her with her homework.

Your mother is so old, in her yearbook Mary and Joseph were voted "Cutest Couple."

Your mother is so old, she uses nylons and a rope for a bra.

Your mother is so old, she knew the Flintstones when they were the New Kids In Bedrock.

Your mother is so old, **THE ONLY THING THAT GETS HER MOVING** is Ex-Lax.

Your mother is so old, she has Jesus Christ trading cards.

Your mother is so old, she's got a wooden bra.

Your father is so old, his face **HAS MORE WRINKLES** than a Sharpei.

YOUR MOTHER IS SO OLD, SHE STARRED IN 'JURASSIC PARK.'

YOUR SISTER IS SO OLD, SHE KNEW ICE CUBE WHEN HE WAS JUST A PUDDLE.

Your father is so old, he said he was at the Crucifixion "JUST HANGIN' AROUND."

Your mother is so old, they needed a crane for her face-lift.

POOR
SNAPS

Your family is so poor, I saw them in a McDonald's parking lot fighting seagulls **FOR FRENCH FRIES.**

Your family is so poor, they put government cheese on layaway.

You're so poor, when I walked into your house and stepped on a penny your father yelled, "Get off my paycheck!"

Your family is so poor, they put Kool-Aid in the toilet so people will think you have **2,000 FLUSHES.**

Your family is so poor, your father took a job cutting grass offshore.

Your family is so poor, the only time **THEY GET NEW APPLIANCES** is after a riot.

Your father is so poor, he carries his food stamps on a money clip.

Your family is so poor, your phone has the employment office on speed dial.

Your mother is so poor, she waves around a Popsicle stick and calls it air conditioning.

Your family is so poor, they wash their **PAPER PLATES.**

YOUR FAMILY IS SO POOR, THEY BUY YOUR CHRISTMAS TREE THE DAY AFTER CHRISTMAS.

87

YOUR FAMILY IS
SO POOR,
YOU GO OUT TO EAT
ONE
AT A TIME.

Your father is so poor, he tried mailing his child support with food stamps.

Your family is so poor, they think **A TWO-INCOME FAMILY** means welfare and food stamps.

Your family is so poor, the only thing you exchanged on Christmas were glances.

You're so poor, you live in a Roach Motel and talk about "livin' large."

You're so poor, you ordered a super-size water at McDonald's.

You're so poor, when I asked why there were holes in your cardboard box you said, "Air conditioning."

You're so poor, you went to the **NINETY-NINE-CENT STORE** and asked for layaway.

Your parents are so poor, for their wedding cake they had frosting on a communion wafer.

Your family is so poor, they put Kool-Aid in your baby bottle.

Your family is so poor, **BOSNIA** sends them money.

YOUR FAMILY IS SO POOR, THEY DON'T HAVE A FAN BUT JUST BLOW ON EACH OTHER.

Your father is so poor, I saw him going sixty-five on the freeway scooping up dead animals on his Big Wheel.

Your family is so poor, at a wedding when the photographer said "cheese" THEY ALL LINED UP.

Your family is so poor, when your grandma died you all fought over her boogers.

SHORT
AND
TALL
SNAPS

Your mother is so short, she has to stand up TO GET DOWN.

Your mother is so short, even AT&T can't reach out and touch her.

Your mother is so short, SHE POLE-VAULTS WITH A TOOTHPICK.

Your father is so tall, he shoots pool with the planets.

Your girlfriend is so short, she said her idols are Arnold and Webster because "she looks up to them."

YOUR ARMS ARE SO SHORT, YOU HAVE TO TILT YOUR HEAD TO SCRATCH YOUR EAR.

Your mother is so short, she thought a dust ball **WAS A TUMBLEWEED**.

Your mother is so short, she has to use a ladder to pick up a dime.

Your mother is so short, she's a professional midget bowler.

Your father is so short, he drives a remote-control car from Radio Shack.

YOUR FATHER IS SO SHORT, he has a job cleaning ankles.

You're so short, you couldn't high-five Smurfs.

YOUR GIRLFRIEND IS SO SHORT, her miniskirt drags.

NASTY

SNAPS

Your mother is so nasty, I called her to fix my VCR because I needed a head cleaner.

Your mother is so nasty, she went swimming and now we have **THE DEAD SEA.**

Your mother is so nasty, she brings crabs to the beach.

Your mother is so nasty, her shit is glad to escape.

Your mother is so nasty, **SHE BRUSHES HER TEETH** with chewing tobacco.

YOUR MOTHER IS SO NASTY, HER CRABS WEAR CONDOMS.

Your mother is so nasty, the last mosquito that bit her got arrested for DWI.

Your sister is so nasty, she must be a tagger because her name is on every street corner.

Your sister is so nasty, she has a sign between her legs: IT'S TROUT SEASON.

Your mother is so nasty, she dries out condoms on the clothesline.

Your mother is so nasty, after sex she asks for free refills.

Your mother is so nasty, you were born out of her ass because her pussy was too busy.

Your family is so nasty, when I asked,"What's for dinner?" they put your sister on the table and said, "Crabs."

Your girlfriend is so nasty, I SAW HER AT A YARD SALE trying on underwear.

YOUR MOTHER IS LIKE A HOCKEY TEAM: SHE CHANGES HER PADS AFTER FOUR PERIODS.

103

COLOR

SNAPS

Your father is so black, he fell down the stairs AND
BURNED RUBBER.

You're so white, you could go to movies as the screen.

Your mother is so ashy, her legs are like spoiled milk—white and
chunky.

You're so white, YOU THINK MARCIA CLARK IS
DOWN.

Your mother is so black, she cries soy sauce.

Your family is so white, they could play tennis naked.

You're so black, IF THEY PUT WHITE DOTS ON YOUR FACE you'd look like a domino.

You're so white, you went out in the snow and they couldn't find you until the spring.

Your father is so black, he can cast a shadow in a coal mine.

You're so white, when you open your mouth I want to DUNK COOKIES INSIDE.

Your mother is so white, at night she gets **A MOON BURN.**

Your mother is so black, she farts smoke.

HAIR
SNAPS

Your dick is so hairy, it looks like the Lion King.

Your mother's lip is so hairy, **SHE WEARS IT IN CORNROWS.**

Your mother has a 'fro with backup lights.

Your mother's so hairy, she went to the beauty parlor to get her back waxed.

Your sister is so ugly, they filmed *GORILLAS IN THE MIST* in her shower.

Your mother is so hairy, her Web site is moms.hairy.com.

Your sister's hair is so nappy, IT LOOKS LIKE A MOP ON CRACK.

Your mother has a metal Afro with rusty sideburns.

YOUR FATHER IS SO BALD, it looks like his neck is blowing bubble gum.

Your mother is so bald, it looks like she's wearing a diaphragm on her head.

YOUR MOTHER IS SO HAIRY, AT BIRTH YOU ALMOST DIED OF RUG BURN.

YOUR MOTHER IS SO
HAIRY,
SHE COULD
DOUBLE FOR
DON KING.

Girl, your hair is so nappy, **WILSON COULDN'T PICKIT.** —MARTIN LAWRENCE, *MARTIN*

Your hair is so short, you couldn't get finger waves, so you got fingerprints.

Your mother is so hairy, she got shot during hunting season.

113

TEETH

SNAPS

Your teeth are so yellow, it looks like **YOU BRUSH WITH CHEEZ WHIZ.**

Your teeth are so yellow, when you open your mouth it's another day.

Your smile is so yellow, it looks like two rows of corn.

Your mother is so toothless, during Halloween she sits on the front porch with a candle in her mouth.

YOUR MOTHER'S MOUTH IS SO ROTTEN, her false teeth have cavities.

Your teeth are so yellow, you can use them as foglights.

Your teeth are so crooked, it looks like someone drove bumper cars in your mouth.

Your girlfriend has got ENOUGH FILM ON HER TEETH to make a movie.

Your teeth are so funky, your mouth looks like a jar of peanut brittle.

Your teeth are so brown, every time people walk by they ask, "What are you eating?"

YOUR TEETH ARE SO CROOKED, THEY LOOK LIKE HUD HOUSING.

Your sister's teeth are so big, she doesn't need braces; she needs railroad tracks.

YOUR FATHER'S MOUTH IS SO ROTTEN,
he can't count to ten on his teeth.

Look at your gums and teeth; it looks like your mother had an affair with Mr. Ed. —DAVE CHAPELLE, *THE NUTTY PROFESSOR*

BIG, SMALL, AND SKINNY SNAPS

Your dick is so small, CRABS USE IT AS A FLAG-POLE.

Your butt is so big, you still can't find your bike.

Your father is so small, he shits pebbles.

Your nose is so big, it makes PINOCCHIO LOOK LIKE A PIGLET.

Your mother's head is so big, she has to use a shopping cart for a hairnet.

Your dick is so small, you use **A RUBBER BAND AND A THIMBLE** and for a jockstrap.

Your mother's head is so big, she has to step into her shirts.

Your mother is so skinny, she stepped on a crack and broke her back.

Your dick is so small, you're hung like a pimple.

Your father's head is so big, **HE NEEDS KICK-STANDS ON EITHER SIDE.**

YOUR MOTHER'S HEAD IS SO BIG, HER SHOWER CAP IS A HEFTY BAG.

Your father's dick is so small, your mom has to use a straw to blow him.

Your mother's tits are so big, they call her the Grand Tetons.

Your girl's hips are so big, people SET THEIR DRINKS ON THEM.

Your mother's head is so big, she has to put on hair spray with a sprinkler.

Your butt is so big, it's got more crack than a drug dealer.

Your mother is so skinny, she snapped her fingers and broke her wrist.

Your girlfriend is so skinny, if she were painted silver she'd look like a parking meter.

Your sister is so small, they use her AS A CHRISTMAS ORNAMENT.

Your sister is so skinny, I can see her heart beating.

Your father is so skinny, he bungee-jumps with dental floss.

Your boyfriend is so small, when he gives you a hickey it looks like a mosquito bite.

Your mother's pussy is so big, you could eat it with a shovel.

Your mother's tits are so small, your father WEARS THE BRA IN THE FAMILY.

Your mother's feet are so big, her shoes have license plates.

Your mother's head is so small, she got her ear pierced and bled to death.

Your mother's head so big, it shows up on radar.

YOUR DICK IS SO SMALL, they call you "needle dick, the bug fucker."

Your lips are so big, you could pull them over your head and wear them as a beanie. —TISHA CAMPBELL, *MARTIN*

SMELLY
SNAPS

Your mother's breath is so smelly, your father kisses her with a stuntman.

Your breath is so hot, it smells like you've got TOE JAM between your teeth.

Your mother's pussy is so stank, cats keep following her around.

Your breath is so bad, you need quadruple mint gum.

Your breath is so bad, it smells like a BAG OF ARMPITS.

—CHRIS ROCK, *MARTIN*

YOU SMELL SO BAD, NOW I KNOW YOU'RE FULL OF SHIT.

129

You stink so bad, your funk has its own body double.

YOUR BREATH IS SO STANK, people look forward to your farts. — DAVE CHAPELLE, *THE NUTTY PROFESSOR*

130

BODY
SNAPS

YOUR MOTHER HAS A SHORT LEG AND WALKS IN CIRCLES

Your sister has no lips, talkin' about "I got **THE KISS OF DEATH.**"

Your mother has no fingers, talking about "I'll point you in the right direction."

Your sister is so flat, she's jealous of the wall.

Your mother has got no left side, talkin' about "she's all right."

Your sister has a glass leg and **LOTIONS IT WITH WINDEX.**

Your brother has one leg and a bicycle.

Your mother has ten fingers—ALL ON THE SAME HAND.

Your mother has a short arm and can't applaud.

Your mother has two wooden legs and ONE IS ON BACKWARDS.

Your mother is so deaf, when I said, "Hey, it's Coolio," she said, "No, it's warm out!"

YOUR MOTHER HAS ONE HAND AND JUST BOUGHT A CLAPPER.

Your mother doesn't have any nipples and they call her smoothy.

Your mother has three fingers and a banjo.

Your mother has a wooden leg WITH BRANCHES.

Your mother is so fat, her blood type is Rocky Road.

—EDDIE MURPHY, *THE NUTTY PROFESSOR*

Your father's face is so wrinkled, IT LOOKS LIKE MY SCROTUM.

HOUSE SNAPS

137

Your house is so old, **THE ONLY THING THAT HOLDS IT UP** is the paint.

Your house is so small, it makes even *your* dick look big.

Your house is so dirty, you have to wipe your feet before you go out.

Your house is so small, when you watch *EIGHT IS ENOUGH,* you can only see four of them.

Your house is so nasty, I walked in and heard the roaches singing "We are family . . ."

YOUR HOUSE

IS SO NASTY, THE SHOWER CURTAIN HAS GRAFFITI.

Your house is so cheap, it looks like you built it during wood shop.

Your house is so nasty, YOU HAVE TO WEAR BOOTS to the bathroom.

Your house is so nasty, at night they put Milk-Bones on your pillow.

Your house is so dirty, when I fell down the stairs I GOT A GREASE STAIN.

Your house is so nasty, when you open the refrigerator the cockroaches throw snowballs at you.

Your house is so small, it's just a ho.

Your house is so cold, **YOU HAVE TO OPEN THE REFRIGERATOR** to keep warm.

Your house is so dirty, the smell of shit makes you homesick.

EYE

SNAPS

You're so blind, you couldn't see my black ass in a room FULL OF MARSHMALLOWS.

Your father's got herpes in his eyes because he's "looking for love in all the wrong places."

Your mother is so cross-eyed, she sees TV in stereo.

Your mother's glasses are SO THICK, she can turn them backwards and tell you what happened yesterday.

You've got one eye, talking about "I'm going to see a double feature."

Your eyes are so big, you have Tupperware contacts.

Your mother is so blind, she stuck her eye up my asshole and STILL COULDN'T SEE SHIT.

SEX
SNAPS

Your sister is so loose, she thinks she's a nun because she's always in the **MISSIONARY POSITION.**

Your sister is so loose, everywhere she goes is easy street.

Your sister is so loose, they throw her baby showers at recess.

Your sister is so loose, I heard the **MILLION MAN MARCH** was a line to her bedroom.

Your father is so horny, when he got locked out of a sex addict meeting he screwed the keyhole.

Your mother is so horny, she tried to blow a statue.

Your mother is so loose, when I called, "Heads or tails?" she said, "I'll give both."

Your mother is so loose, when God was **GIVING OUT BRAINS** she was giving Joseph head.

Your mother is like a police station: Dicks go in all day and night.

Your sister is so loose, she's a trisexual: Name any kind of sex, and she's tried it.

YOUR SISTER IS SO LOOSE, HER WEB SITE IS WWW.COME.COM.

148

Your sister is just like Nintendo: You can play her with your joystick.

Your sister is so easy, after sex she moves to the front seat for a smoke.

Your mother is like **AN EASY GOLF COURSE:** Everyone can get a hole in one.

Your sister is so loose, when she walks down the street her pussy claps.

Your father is like a squirrel: **HE PICKS HIS NUTS.**

Your mother is so loose, when she got a new miniskirt everyone said, **"NICE BELT."**

Your sister is so loose, she has a guest book hanging on her belt.

Your mother is so loose, it took her ten times to get a driver's license because she couldn't get used to the front seat.

Your girl's pussy is like a Navy ship—**FULL OF SEMEN.**

Your mother is so easy, she has her legs open on the front of a Wheaties box saying, "Breakfast of Champions."

Your mother is so loose, she held a "Hands Across My Ass" charity drive.

Your mother is so loose, she wears her vibrators on **A TOOL BELT.**

Your girl is so loose, she gets discounts at the abortion clinic.

Your sister is so loose, when they asked how she liked her eggs she said, **"FERTILIZED."**

Your mother is so loose, she's blind and seeing another man.

Your mother is so loose, she wears knee pads and yells,
"CURB SERVICE!"

Your mother is so horny, she'd hump a pole if it had pants on.

Your mother is so loose, when they asked if she was ready for her driving test she said, "Hop on."

Your mother is so loose, I went to your house and said, "Let me in," so she PULLED DOWN HER PANTIES.

Your mother is like a pinball machine: Everybody gets their balls off.

YOUR GIRL IS SO NASTY, I PUT A GLOVE ON JUST TO WAVE TO HER.

Your sister is a great ballplayer; she plays with my balls every chance she gets.

Your sister is so horny, **SHE BOUGHT SEVEN CUCUMBERS AND** labeled them "Monday Night," "Tuesday Night," "Wednesday Night . . . "

Your sister is so loose, she thinks safe sex is locking the car door.

Your sister is so loose, she uses the Washington Monument as a dildo.

Your mother has more positions than a Craftmatic Adjustable Bed.

Your mother is so horny, **SHE'S SEEN MORE DICK** than a urinal at a Greyhound station.

Your mother sucks so much dick, her tongue has jock itch.

Your sister is like a basketball, getting bounced from one brother to the next.

Your sister gets ridden so much, she has a **SIX FLAGS TATTOO** on her butt.

Your brother is so gay, they call him "famous anus."

YOUR SISTER IS SO EASY, I got a night with her at the Ninety-Nine-Cent store.

Your mother is like a bottle of ketchup: She gets turned over, banged, and then comes slow.

SNAP

SHOTS

ILLUSTRATED BY KENT GAMBLE

SNAP SHOTS UGLY SNAPS

YOUR SISTER IS SO UGLY, SHE'S A
HOSTESS AT A ROACH MOTEL

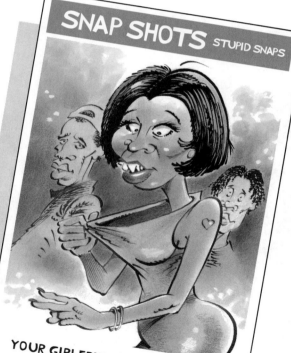

SNAP SHOTS STUPID SNAPS

YOUR GIRLFRIEND IS SO STUPID,
SHE HAS TO LOOK DOWN HER
BLOUSE TO COUNT TO TWO.

MAIL
BAG

THANKS TO THESE SNAPPERS FROM ACROSS THE COUNTRY WHO SENT IN THEIR FAVORITE SNAPS, CAPS, AND DISSES FOR US TO INCLUDE IN SNAPS 4:

GREG AARONS
Evanston, IL

ABRAXAS FOUNDATION
Waverly, WV

JASON ALEXANDER
Hazlet, NJ

BILL ALSTON
Binghamton, NY

ALAA-HAMAOUI
Alexandria, VA

LARRY AGPAOA
Lihue, HI

SCOTT AKINS
Neptune City, NJ

RICHARD ALONSO
Kennewick, WA

BRANDI BRITT
Olathe, KS

CHRIS BYRD
Pinehurst, NC

FERRELL BANKS
Chicago, IL

NIKKI BANNISTER
Norfolk, VA

IAN BERNAR
Middletown, RI

TIA BLAIR
Richmond Hill, NY

B. BLAKELY
Providence, RI

ELI BLOSHTEIN
Bronx, NY

BRENT BOCIAN
Naples, FL

JOSEPH D. BOYD
Wheeling, IL

JACQUI BRACCO
Fort Lee, NJ

BRANDON BRADLEY
Plain City, OH

JEFF BROWN
Cincinnati, OH

MARC BROWN
San Jose, CA

LINDA E. BRYANT
Greenshow, NC

SMITCHA BURANASOMBATI
Los Angeles, CA

WILLIAM BURNS
Linwood, CT

GUSTAVO CANTELIANO
Corona, CA

JOHN CAPRARO
Utica, NY

DREW CARRIE
Des Moines, IA

GLEN CARAMBAS
Carson, CA

SEAN CARTER
Yonkers, NY

DAN CARUSO
Barre, MA

FRANK CANO
Covina, CA

JERALD CHAVEZ
Union City, CA

STAFFORD CHESTIN
Graterford, PA

JON CHING
Kapoa, HI

ANTHONY COLLINS
Springfield, MA

JACOB COLBATH
El Cajon, CA

JERRELL COLVIN
Seattle, WA

JEFFREY COOPER
Rochester, NY

B. CRANGLE
Syracuse, NY

RYAN CROSBY
Virginia Beach, VA

ANTHONY CRUZ
Compton, CA

ECHO CURRY
Tacoma, WA

JAL DANIEL
Antioch, CA

DAMIAN DAUILA
McAllen, TX

DIANA DAVIS
Jamaica Plain, MA

CHARLES DETMAR
Greensboro, NC

JEREMY TODD DIAMOND
Silver Spring, MD

JASON DIXIE
Fort Wayne, IN

JEFF DOUGLAS
Brooklyn, NY

MIKE DORAN
Cos Cob, CT

CURT DUELL
Scottsdale, AZ

KEVIN DUKES
St. Louis, MO

KURT R. DUGGINS
Stillwater, OK

RYAN DIPRIZIO
Union, NH

SKOT DRUCKER
North Miami Beach, FL

CURT DUELL
Scottsdale, AZ

TERESA DIAZ
Windham, CT

DINH DIEP
Monterey Park, CA

BRIAN ELAM
Lecanta, FL

CHRIS ESPINA
Springfield, VA

CARLOS ESTRADA
Santa Barbara, CA

LADONNA ETHRIDGE
Detroit, MI

SHAMAL EVANS
New York, NY

161

GEORGE FETTER
Tampa, FL

JONATHAN FELDMAN
Philadelphia, PA

MARK FELDMAN
Yonkers, NY

TRAVIS FESLER
Wichita, KS

ALEX FIGUEROA
Frederick, MD

EDWARD T. FLOUNOY
Brooklyn, NY

DAVID FORESTIER
Orlando, FL

KENYM FOSTER
Bradford, MA

LOWELL FRANKLIN
Oakland, CA

BILL FRYE
Weston, WV

MARIA FUENTES
Oxnard, CA

AARON GARCIA
McAllen, TX

CRYSTAL GARRETT
Lexington, KY

JESSE GAVETTE
Hubert, NC

CORI GEROU
Munising, MI

JEFFREY GIORDANO
Williamstown, NJ

DENISE GONZALEZ
Cicero, IL

JONNY GONZALEZ
El Paso, TX

JOEY GUERRERO
Corpus Christi, TX

SHARON HASSEL
Chicago, IL

POONAM HEMLANI
Tam, Guam

VINCENT HILL
Little Rock, AR

WILLY HILL
North Philadelphia, PA

GREG HOLCOMB
Fredonia, WI

MIKE HOLOWAY
Covington, LA

ROB HOUSE
Freeport, NY

ANDY HOWARD
Madison, AL

BILL HUNTER
West Hartford, CT

MIKE JACOB
Westport, CT

PAUL JAKUBONSKI, JR.
Bayonne, NJ

WILLIAM JARRETT, JR.
Providence, RI

JOSE JIMENEZ
Vallejo, CA

LEE JOHNSON
Salieta, CA

KKAPK
Baltimore, MD

PJ KAPSALES
Woodinville, WA

MARISA KAVANAUGH
Hampton, VA

MATT WILLIAM
KELLEMAN
Pittson, PA

TRACOYIA KEGLER
AND KIWANIS
MOSLEY
Albany, GA

SHAWN KENNEY
Brunswick Hills, OH

ROBERT M. KERN
Yonkers, NY

KEVIN KEYS
Brooklyn, NY

LARRY KING
New York, NY

WAYNE KING
Sleepy Hollow, NY

OLIVER LANAUX, JR.
Oakland, CA

ALBERT LARKINS
Tampa, FL

NATHAN LEWIS
Spencer, IN

CHRIS LIBERTO
Littleton, CO

ERIC LINDSAY
Westfield, MA

SUKITA LINDSEY
Rocky Mount, NC

JILLIAN LIPPMAN
Newton, CT

KRISTA LOWE
Hooper, UT

SEAN LOVELAC
Detroit, MI

TONY LOPEZ
Kress, TX

JUSTIN LUCAS
San Francisco, CA

MELISSA MAASKE
Newark, DE

ARTHUR McCALL
Brooklyn, NY

JOHNNY
MACDONALD
Jamaica, NY

CAMILLE McGEE
East St. Louis, IL

CONNIE McGOWAN
Quitman, MS

COE MOE D
McKENZIEL
Big Sandy, TX

BETHANY MACNEUR
Beaverton, OR

CURTIS McVAUGHN
Jayess, MS

ED MADRIGAL
Olathe, KS

GRIFFIN MARKS
Merrimack, NH

MARTHA MARCH
Lexington, MS

AKEEM MARSH
Bronx, NY

ARCHIE MARTIU
Pulaski, VA

RHONDA MATHEWS
Milledgeville, GA

NATASHA MATHIS
Manchester, CA

BILL MAURIZIO
Pittsburgh, PA

TED MERRIMAN
Radnor, PA

LAWAN MITCHELL
Detroit, MI

162

TERESA MITCHELL
Woodland, CA

JAMES MOORE III
Philadelphia, PA

CRAIG MORVANT
Metairie, LA

DESI MOTLEY
FPO AP

MOLLY MYERS
Brooklyn, NY

ROBERT NEDELL
Winfield, NY

ROB NEDELL
Herkimer, NY

ALEX NESS
Sunnyvale, CA

A. J. NEVILL
Roseville, CA

BRENDAN NIES
North Aurora, IL

DANIEL NOEL
Arlington, MA

DUMISANI NOLOUU
Blacksbury, VA

JEFF NOVER
Pembroke Pines, FL

JOHNNY OCHOA
Sacramento, CA

HOLLY O'KEEFE
Forestdale, MA

JOSEPH OLIN
Miami Beach, FL

MARK ONIAS
Oxnard, CA

OSCAR ORTEGA
New York, NY

SONJA PALMER
Des Moines, IA

AL PARKS
El Paso, TX

JUSTIN PARTRIDGE
Calera, AL

ALMAR PASCUA
Santa Clara, CA

PAWS
Paterson, NJ

RAYMOND PEREZ
Houston, TX

JONATHAN PERRY III
Charlotte, NC

ANGELE PETTERSON
Eatontown, NJ

MARK PHILLIPS
Bronx, NY

JACK PHOPNICHITH
San Francisco, CA

MARVIN PIARD
Elmont, NY

CHUCK PURNELL
Dover, DE

RICH QUIGLEY
Seattle, WA

LAKECIA RAMEY
Henderson, NV

EDER RAMIREZ
Bronx, NY

JASON RAMPY
Missoula, MT

NICK RASLEY
Sparks, NV

JUD REED
Stafford, VA

RENE REYNOSO
San Bernardino, CA

TRENT REZNOR
Zanesville, OH

CHRIS RHOAD
Marion, OH

BENNY RICCARDO
Levittown, NY

YERANIA RIVAZ
Sun Valley, NV

FRANK RIVERA
New Paltz, NY

RANDY ROBINSON
Security, CO

ROSENDO
RODRIGUEZ
Mathis, TX

VANESSA
RODRIGUEZ
Hialeah, FL

LARRY ROLLINS, JR.
Frederick, MD

ANDRETTI ROTT
San Antonio, TX

D. W. SAGER
Jamestown, ND

DAVID SANDERS
Spanaway, WA

NICKY SANDOVAL
Woodland, CA

DAVID SAPIGAO
Glendale, CA

ROBERT SCHNEIDER
Wrightsville, CA

JODAN SCOTT
Rodger, AK

QUANDRAY SCOTT
Florence, SC

J. D. SHELTON
Centreville, VA

D. SHELLAN
Monterey, CA

SGT. JOHNSON
SERRY
USAREUR, APO AE

WAYNE SHOOK
Bolton Landing, NY

FRANCIS SIERRA
San Diego, CA

TRAVIS SILMAN
Marietta, GA

CHARISE SIMMONS
South Orange, NJ

CHARLES SIMSTROM
Rockford, IL

PETER SIMSTROM
Rockford, IL

WAYMON SISK
Memphis, TN

JOHN SMITH
Ambler, PA

SAMUEL SMITH
Irma, WI

WAYNE SMITH
Flint, MI

CHRIS SMYLIE
Ione, CA

GUILLERMO SOTO
Miami, FL

CHAWNDRA
SPALIONE
Glendora, CA

SHALOND SPANN
Hilton Head, SC

XIMENA STERLING
Brooklyn, NY

J. STEVENS
Circleville, OH

KENDRICK SUMTER
South Carolina

163

DENVER TANGONAN
Saipan, MP

TANYA TAYLOR
Riverside, CA

CEDRIC TATE
Las Vegas, NV

SOEUN TEK
San Francisco, CA

JOSH THROWER
Colorado Springs, CO

EVAN TRAVITSKY
Altamont Springs, FL

STEPHANIE TRAVITSKY
Brooklyn, NY

T TROUPE
Topeka, KS

VALINE TUCKER
Jersey City, NJ

TIFFANY TURNIPSEED
Oakland, CA

AMANDA VENTURA
Las Vegas, NV

HECTOR VILLAGOMEZ
Soledad, CA

JESSICA VILLATORO
Los Angeles, VA

CLIFFORD L. VIRADOR
Chicago, IL

JESSE WAITE AND NATHAN ENEY
Bothell, WA

JACOB WARNER
Denver, CO

JEANIE WARREN
Sacramento, CA

MYKON WASHINGTON
Randallstown, MD

MICHAEL WAY
Bronx, NY

SHAWN WEAKISS
Chicago, IL

JACQUELINE WHITE
Dallas, TX

LORNA WHITE
North Miami, FL

ANITA WILLIAMS
Buffalo, NY

BILL WILLIAMS
Cookeville, TN

RANDY WILLIAMS
Bradenton, FL

KEVIN WILLIAMS
Oxon Hill, MD

RAYNARD WILLIAMS
Los Angeles, CA

FRED WOLFF
Bellflower, CA

SAM WORTHEN
Arlington, VA

WILLIAM YOUMANS
Moorpark, CA

164

AND PROPS TO THESE ALL-STAR SNAPPERS FOR HELPING MAKE OUR PREVIOUS BOOKS THE BOMB:

MICHAEL ADAMS
Bremen, IN

NICK ADELL
Madison, WI

KEKAILANI AIU
Honolulu, HI

TODD ALEXANDER
Columbus, OH

RICHARD ALONSO
Kennewick, WA

BILL ALSTON
Binghamton, NY

ROBERT AMBROZE
Pasadena, CA

DEREK ANSAM
Honolulu, HI

CHRISTOPHER ARENA
New Brunswick, NJ

ROY F. ATIZADO
Seattle, WA

JASON ATKINSON
Indianapolis, IN

LINDA AZEVEDO
White Plains, NY

SHAWN BANASAN
Dover, DE

ALFREDO BANUELOS
Modesto, CA

BOE BECKER AND JOHN PRELESKI
Plainville, CT

RICK BECKER
Stow, MA

ALFRED BEDONIA
Delano, CA

SARAH BELFORD
Montrose, MI

MATT BELLGRAPH
Binghamton, NY

TONY BERRY
Brighton, UK

JAIME BERTAN
Mission Viejo, CA

PETE BEUTTELL
Titusville, FL

DAVID BRID
Manteca, CA

DOUG BLACK
Birmingham, AL

LUCAS A. BOHN
Matthews, VA

JUSTIN BORUCKI
Chicago, IL

JASON BOSCHERT
APO, AE

VALENCIA BOSON
San Diego, CA

KAREN BROWN
Oceanside, CA

BRIAN BURGHOUT
Glendale, AZ

KARLA BURGUENO
Fresno, CA

NOAH BURNETT
East Palo Alto, CA

JOHN CAPRARO
Utica, NY

BECKY CHARITON
Concord, MA

BRIAN CHIN
Flushing, NY

JON CHING
Kapaa, HI

TREVOR CLARK
Brooklyn, NY

ADRIENNE COLA
Las Vegas, NV

JACOB COLBATH
San Diego, CA

RICK COLLINS
Dearborn Heights, MI

ROBERT COLLINS
Brooklyn, NY

JOY COLTER
Rock Hill, SC

BEN CONNELLY
Fort Wayne, IN

CHRIS CONTAOI
San Bernardino, CA

ANTHONY CONTI
Bayside, NY

JOSEPH CONTRENAS
Covina, CA

JEFFREY COOPER
Rochester, NY

ROSE "BAMBAM" COOPER
Lansing, MI

BOBBY CORD
Clinton, MD

BILL CRAIG
Chattanooga, TN

RON CUNNINGHAM
Peru, IN

ANDREW CURRIE
Des Moines, IA

AMANDA DEATON
Trenton, OH

DANIEL DEIS
Marina, CA

CHRIS DIAZ
Sharon, PA

JASON DIXIE
Fort Wayne, IN

MARCOS DOMICIANO
Union, NJ

MATT DORMAN
Las Vegas, NV

KURT R. DUGGINS
Stillwater, OK

CURT DUELL
Scottsdale, AZ

CHIP DU PONT
Fishers Island, NY

CHRISTOPHER ECK
Worcester, MA

STEPHAN EGBERT
Orland Park, IL

BRIAN L. ELAM
Lecamto, FL

BRANDON ELLIOTT
Virginia Beach, VA

VINNIE ESPARZA
Oakland, CA

LADONNA ETHERIDGE
Detroit, MI

BRANDON EVANS
Redondo Beach, CA

GEORGE FETTER
Tampa, FL

RONNIE FLORENTE
Visalia, CA

DAVID FRANCE
University of Connecticut, Storrs, CT

HENRY F. FRANKE, JR.,
Waden, NY

LA KESHA FRAZIER
Reno, NV

SAM GAGLIANO
Rochester, NY

GIOVANNI GALLUZZO
Stamford, CT

ANDY GAMEZ
Blythe, CA

AARON GARCIA
McAllen, TX

CHRISTOPHER GARCIA
Hammond, IN

JILLIAN ASHLEY GELD
Elkins Park, PA

MICHAEL GLICK
Scarsdale, NY

MATT GOODWIN
Ardsley, NY

DAMARIA GREEN
San Jose, CA

DAVE GREENFIELD
New York, NY

BRADLEY GROVER
Winchester, NH

JOE GRAZER
Allentown, PA

MEGHAN A. HAFEMAN
Pembine, WI

IAN HALL
Weston, WV

GEOFFREY HARLEY
Chicago, IL

CARTER HARRIS
Tolland, CT

MIKE HASS
Eureka, CA

IAN HERMAN
Staten Island, NY

LUIS HERNANDEZ
Bronx, NY

CHRIS B-HILL
Hartsdale, NY

DEREK HIRONS
Fiskdale, MA

LESLIE HITTEL
Brockton, MA

NATALIE HOBSON
Richmond, TX

DALLAS LEE HOLGUIN
Venice, CA

LAVALLE HOUSER
Dallas, TX

SHERRY HOWARD
Blakely, GA

CHRISTIAN HUGES
Hopkinsville, KY

ROBIE HUNGERFORD AND TRAVIS HAWKINS
Reading, CA

165

ELLIOT JOHNSON
Winnetka, IL

CHRIS JONES
Portage, MI

D. JONES
Indianapolis, IN

LINDSEY MARIE JONES
Bailey, NC

JASON M. KAUMANS
Belmond, IA

SUSIE KELLER
Cincinnati, OH

TODD KEYES
New Orleans, LA

WARREN KLARMAN, JR.
Inverness, FL

CHRIS KOFOL
Bronxville, NY

KENTON KOGA
Pearl City, HI

GLENN KROLL
Great Neck, NY

BRIAN KUHN
Grand Junction, CO

JOE LAM
Collings Lakes, NJ

JIM LARSE
Greenville, OH

MICHAEL AND JORDAN LEFF
Bedford, NY

MORRIE H. LEW
Rolling Hills, CA

LOUIS ST. LEWIS
Chapel Hill, NC

JAMES LITTLEJOHN
Texarkana, TX

TIM LOEBBAKA
Mount Prospect, IL

TONY LOO
Seattle, WA

RENANN LOPEZ
Daly City, CA

ANTWAIN LOVE
Chicago, IL

KRISTA LOWE
Hooper, UT

RAY LUGO
New York, NY

CHRIS LUMPKIN
San Diego, CA

JOHNNY MA
San Jose, CA

ALVIN L. McCARVER III
Chicago, IL

JONATHAN McGRAW
Bloomfield Hills, MI

STEVE McKEE
Warrington, PA

MICHELLE McKINNON
Las Vegas, NV

MAC McMURRAY
Lake Worth, FL

BETHANY MACNEUR
Beaverton, OR

RODERICK MACUGAY
Lihue Kauai, HI

SCOTT MADDUX
Albuquerque, NM

LISA MANESCU
Bethlehem, PA

NICK MANJARREZ
Wapato, WA

MARK MANN
Ridgewood, NY

JOSH MARTIN
Cedar Rapids, IA

JESSE MASON
Cape Girardeau, MO

RHONDA MATHEWS
Milledgeville, GA

MASHADI MATABANE
Capitol Heights, MD

MIGUEL MATOS
New York, NY

BUBBA MAYS
Aviston, IL

JOSH MAYWALT
Knoxville, TN

ADAM MEAGHER
Revere, MA

MANNY MEDINA
North Haven, CT

MELISSA MEGAS
Albany, NY

JILL MENECKER
Bayside, NY

DERRICK MILENKOFF
Hobart, IN

NICK MINIER
Lafayette, NY

BERNY MITCHELL
Philadelphia, PA

KIYOMI MIZUKAMI
FPO, AP

LILLIAN K. MOLL
Los Angeles, CA

SEAN MONAHAN
Mililani, HI

ALEXIS MONTOYA
Woodland, CA

LORI MOONEY
Bronx, NY

DEREK MUCKELROY
Kilgore, TX

SEBASTIAN MURESAN
Modesto, CA

MATTHEW MURPHY
Kirkland, WA

DAVID MYRICK
Monterey, CA

BRAD NACIO
Gretna, LA

DANIEL NADOLSKI
New Britain, CT

TYLER NORBY
Portland, OR

YANDI NUNEZ
Hialeah, FL

JEFF OBAYASHI
San Diego, CA

JON OH
Torrance, CA

CHRISTOPHER MIGUEL OLIVARES
Oakland, CA

SHARRIEFF OMAR
Germantown, MD

DEREK ORCHARD
Reno, NV

JESSIE ORTIZ
Wapato, WA

NATALIE M. PADILLA
Santa Barbara, CA

N. PARGHI
Martinez, GA

LONNIE PARKER
Dunbar, WV

ALMAR PASCUA
Santa Clara, CA

MARK PASCUA
Daly City, CA

KEVIN PAUL
Burbank, CA

SEAN PENN
Highland, NJ

HOLMES POOSER
Reno, NV

RANDY PORTER
Belmont, MA

KIM POWELL
Kankakee, IL

CHARLES CRIPPEN-PROPHET
Philadelphia, PA

SKOT PRUCKER
North Miami Beach, FL

DANNY PUENTE
San Antonio, TX

MATT RADER
Weatouge, CT

MICHAEL RAGASA
Wailuku, HI

MATTHEW RAY
Harrisburg, PA

TARA J. RAY
Fontana, CA

BECKY REUSS
Pierce, NE

DAVID RICHARD
Clarksburg, WV

DUSTY RICHIE
Cincinnati, OH

DANETON RIVERA
Coplay, PA

DEBBIE ROAQUIN
Glendale, NY

MORGAN ROCKEY
Maple Valley, WA

ANNIE ROMO
Santa Barbara, CA

CIANE RUSSELL
Roanoke, VA

ANGELLA SAAVEDRA
Queens, NY

DAVID SALING
New Orleans, LA

JENNIFER SALINAS
White Plains, NY

KAARON SAPHIR
New York, NY

DEREK SAUNDERS
Evansville, IN

KATIE SCHAFFER
North Tonawanda, NY

MONICA SCOTT
Cincinnati, OH

COVAR SEARS
Bethlehem, PA

KEN "LIZARD" SHEIDE
Okinawa City, Japan

PETER SIDLOVSKY
Farmington, CT

KIMBERLY SILVA
Keaau, HI

JESSICA SILVERTHRONE
Washington, DC

DONALD SMILEY
Charlotte, NC

KIMBERLINE SMITH
Hawthorne, CA

RICHARD C. STANGE
Philadelphia, PA

NATHAN STEVEN
Dubuque, IA

CHAPIN STRONG
Granada Hills, CA

MASULAH SURMATY
Burke, VA

DAN SWEET
Kingston, RI

BRIAN SZAFRANSKI
Port St. Joe, FL

CHRISTINA TALIAFERROW
Brooklyn, NY

ALEX TAMAYO
El Centro, CA

CHRIS TOBIA
New Haven, CT

JUSTIN TODD
Memphis, TN

STEVEN TONG
Alameda, CA

JOHNATHAN TORRES
New York, NY

LYDIA TOTH
Sunnyvale, CA

PAUL TRAN
Starling, VA

MIKE TRATNIK
Fresno, CA

JIM TRINH
Egan, MN

KIM TROUPE
Topeka, KS

BRIAN TYLER
Shelbyville, KY

FRANKLIN VASQUEZ
Daly City, CA

ANDREA VELAZQUEZ
Staten Island, NY

CHARLES R. WELCH
Charlotte, NC

AARON WERMAN
Atlantic Beach, NY

LINDY WHEATLEY
Champaign, IL

JAMES WHEELER
Hailey, ID

MICHAEL WILBEKIN
Bronx, NY

DAVE WILSON
Crown Point, IN

FRED WOLFF
Bellflower, CA

LISA YOUNT
El Cerrito, CA

JOESPH YRULEGUI
Fresno, CA

WILLIAM ZARATE
Lynwood, CA

168 ACKNOWLEDGMENTS

THANKS TO THE FOLLOWING PEOPLE FOR THEIR CREATIVE CONTRIBUTIONS AND SUPPORT:

Vincent Anelle • The Axelrods • H. Beale Co. • Dr. Michael Braver • Pat DeRosa • Rudy Durand • Bruce Feinberg • Austin Hearst • Bruce Hill • Ice-T • Homer Jolly • David J. Leiter • Brad Marks • Quincy Jones • Jim McGee • Andy Nulman • Bruce Paisner • Lew Perlman • Alan Potashnick • Jon Rubin • Mary Salter • Gary Sharfin • James Signorelli • Alan and Anita Sosne • Yalda Tehranian • Frank Wolf

AND THANKS TO THOSE WHO CAN SNAP EVEN BETTER THAN WE CAN . . .

Dr. John Abroon • Sharon Alexander • Edward Anderson II • Mercedes Ayala • Jimbo Barnett • Elana Barry • Rob Bartlet • Bart Bartolomeo • Michael Blumenthal • Eric Boardman • Buckanla • Donna Campbell • Sharron Cannon • L. Judith Carroll • Marc Chamlin, Esq • George Ciccarone • Cloudy Brothers: Skipper Davis, Keith Heard, Little Tiny Heard, Jimmy Kennedy, Doug Curtiss • Chris Cohen • Yvette Coit • Anthony Cooper, Jr. • Lauren Correo • Bob Craft • Eric Daniel • Mary Edwards • Diana Farmer • Randy Fechter • Monica Fox • Roy Frumkes • Renee Glicker • Dr. Steven Glickman • Shannon Goulding • Tina Graham • Carole Green, Esq • Bruce Grivetti • Dr. Duane Grummons • Mike and Joellyn Haddad • Trip Hargrave III • Jennifer Heard • Amy Henkels • Doug Herzog • Chester Higgins, Jr. • Dave Holbrook • Jordan Horowitz • Cella Irvine • Susie Israelson • Mark Itken • Waverly Ivey • Jezebel Restaurant • Tammi K. Jones • Geoffry Juviler • Ilene Kahn • William Keller • Barry and BettyLou Kibrick • Kline & Friends • Kevin Labick, Mercury 7 • Patricia Lawrence • Phil Lebovitz • Daniel Lehmann • Gary Lennon • Lenny's • Michael Lewittes • Soo Long • Chester Mapp • Rick Messina • Tracy Moore • Bob Moses and Noreen O'Loughlin • Jim Pasternak • Shawn Marie Richardz • Bob Risse • Jaimie Roberts, Esq. • Dan Rosen • Lawrence Rosenthal • Jeff Ross • Hillary Rushnell • Jon Sanpietrov • Mike Sargent • Brent Saunders • Jessica Schwartz • Mitch Semel • Shark Bar • Eric Solstein • Soul Cafe • Jason Steinberg • Joel Stillerman • Kevin Swain • Dr. Gary Takowsky • Keith Truesdell • Jeffrey Uvezian • David Vigliano • Wheeler-Sussman • Doreen Whitten • Richard Winkler • Barbara Zitware Agency •

AND HUGE THANKS TO THE SUPPORT OF SOME OF AMERICA'S LEADING COMEDY CLUBS:

Boston Comedy Club	Barry Katz	New York City
Caroline's Comedy Club and Comedy Nation	Caroline Hirsch	New York City
Catch a Rising Star	Rick Newman/William Mclaughlin	New York City
Comic Strip	Lucen Hold	New York City
Gotham Comedy Club	Chris Mazzilli and Michael Reisman	New York City
Monty's Comedy Crib	Monteria Ivey	New York City
Standup New York	Cary Hoffman	New York City
Comedy Act Theatre	Michael Williams	Los Angeles
The Townhouse	Hope Flood	Los Angeles
The Funnybone	Dee Lee and Mike Bailey	Philadelphia
B's Comedy Kitchen	Leslie Rodgers and Steve Maminga	Detroit
Hip Hop Comedy Stop	Rushaion McDonald and David Raibon	Houston
Monique's Comedy Club	Steven Imes	Baltimore
The Sugar Kane Club	Charles Kane	Washington, D.C.
Bugsby's Spotlight	Wendell Rush	Birmingham

HERE'S A SHOUT TO JUST SOME OF THE COMEDIANS WHO ARE KEEPING IT REAL:

Arceneaux & Mitchell

Arnold Acevedo

Benny B

Greer Barnes

Jeff Brown

Sam Brown

D.C. Benny

Mike B.

Bill Bellamy

Mike Blackson

Jim Breuer

Xavier Cadeau

Franz Caseaus

Dave Chapelle

Joe Claire

Cedric the Entertainer

Michael Epps

Faceman

Faison

Fig Man

FLEX

Derrick Fox

Andrew Fraiser

Ardie Fuqua

Big Warren Gardner

Garfield

Amazing Grace

Adele Givens

Eddie Griffin

James T. Harris

Terry Hodges

Monteria Ivey

Anthony "A.J." Johnson

Alonzo Hamburger Jones

Cortez Jackson

A. J. Jamal

Capital J

Gerald Kelly

T. K. Kirkland

Master Lee

Cathy Lewis

Toothless Lover

Bernie Mac

Uncle Jimmy Mack

Macio

Johnny Mae

Tracy Morgan

Carlos Mencia

Rudy Rae Moore

Mugga

Most Brothers

Scott Paparcuri

Ray Ray

Freddie Ricks

Rudy Rush

Snick

Rickey Smiley

Brooklyn Mike Smith

Forever Smooth

J. B. Smoove

Somore

T-Rex

Talent

Chris Tucker

Sheryl Underwood

Rich Vos

A. G. White

Wil

Tony Woods

THESE DJs ARE SO DUMB, THEY WEAR BATHING SUITS TO WORK IN CASE THEY GET HIT BY RADIO WAVES:

Alex Bennett Show	KITS	San Francisco, CA
Zoo Crew	KMEL-FM	San Francisco, CA
Rick Chase Show	KMEL	San Francisco, CA
Mike Chase	KDON	Salinas, CA
DJ Nalver	KWIN	Stockton, CA
Willis Johnson Show	KKDA-AM	Dallas, TX
Skip Murphey	KKDA-FM	Dallas, TX
Day Time Magazine	KKDA	Dallas, TX
Cousin Lenny	KKDA	Dallas, TX
Mike Sargent	WBAI	New York, NY
The David Brenner Show	Westwood One	New York, NY
Mark Riley	WLIB	New York, NY
The Mike Walker Show	Westwood One	New York, NY
Dre and Lover Show	Hot 97	New York, NY
Michele Wright and Bat Johnson	WBLS	New York, NY
Trent Taylor	WAXQ	New York, NY
Christine Nagy	WAXQ	New York, NY
Salim Mwakhu	WVON-AM	New York, NY
Lukas	Z100	New York, NY
Big John Tobin	WPDH	Poughkeepsie, NY
The Wolf	WPDH	Poughkeepsie, NY
Mad Mike	WPDH	Poughkeepsie, NY
Brother Weuse	WZMF AM	Rochester, NY
Backstage Press	WBEZ (NPR)	Chicago, IL
John Walk	WVON-AM	Chicago, IL
Johnny Vohn	WLS	Chicago, IL
Hot Ice in the Afternoon	WCLK-FM	Atlanta, GA
Morning Show	WIBB-FM	Atlanta, GA
Bernie McCain Show	WOL-AM	Washington, D.C

Jones & Co.	WMMJ	Washington, D.C.
Larence Gregory Jones	WMMS	Washington, D.C.
Dave & Brian	WUSL	Philadelphia, PA
Nick Talifero	WHAT-AM	Philadelphia, PA
Mike & Carol Show	WVEE	Atlanta, GA
Hot Ice in the Afternoon	WCLK-FM	Atlanta, GA
Mark Nelson	WROV	Huntsville, AL
Steve Johnson	WEZB	New Orleans, LA
Gary Spears	WEZB	New Orleans, LA
Sam Giles	WROV	Roanoke, VA
Mark Nelson	WROV	Roanoke, VA
Jeff Oh	WROV	Roanoke, VA
Rick Barber Show	KOA-AM	Denver, CO
Big Dave and The Duke	WKDF	Nashville, TN
Scott Overton	CIGM	Ontario, Canada

ABOUT THE AUTHOR

JAMES PERCELAY is a comedy writer and producer who was a former development executive at Hearst Entertainment and film producer at Saturday Night Live. He is currently developing SNAPS into a motion picture, writing a new humor book series, and producing a youth-oriented SNAPS anti-smoking campaign for the American Cancer Society.

We would like your comments on this book,

as well as your favorite original snaps.

If we include your new snaps in our next book,

we'll acknowledge your contributions.

2 BROS &

A WHITE GUY

P.O. Box 764

Planetarium Station

New York, NY 10024-0539